How to be a Successful Introvert

I0422171

Kendra Wilson

Table of Contents

Author's Note:

Hello,
This is the part of the book where I am supposed to start talking about myself, Ironically, I have a hard time talking about myself.

My name is Kendra Wilson and I enjoy helping people with their problems and promoting a healthy lifestyle. I am always exploring healthy diet alternatives and addressing issues that I can relate to.

I am a bit of a homebody. Besides writing, I enjoy watching television , eating healthy foods and drinking a nice bottle of wine. I really hope my books are helping people.

Sincerely,
Kendra Wilson

Introduction

Being an introvert is something that many people think is a bad thing. They think of someone who just wants to sit at home all of the time and never talk to others ever. This might seem strange to those who like to be out all of the time, but being an introvert is not such a bad thing. In fact, some of the most successful people have been introverts. I have been an introvert my whole life and while it may be a little strange when I would like to sit back and just read a book or hang out with my family rather than going out and partying all of the time, that is who I am and that is what I enjoy doing.

I have written this guidebook as a way to help you understand that despite the prevalent views on this kind of personality, being an introvert is not a bad thing. I have been this kind of person my whole life and it has never held me back from making some amazing friends, having a great family, traveling the world, and even starting my own business. And now I want to use this guidebook to share some of the interesting tips and tricks that I have learned throughout my life as an introvert.

I started out with chapter 1 being about why it is such a good thing to be an introvert. I thought this would help you to see that while you may be a bit quieter and like to do things on your own sometimes, there is still so much of value when it comes to being you. First off, you are smart, easy to get along with, responsible and can be counted on all of the time, and you can combine creative and analytical thinking in ways that others are envious of. You bring a lot to the table and learning that was one of the hardest things I had to figure out when I made my path in life.

Next I will spend some time talking with you about how you can be an introvert and still be successful in the work place. Some of the best workers in the world are introverts and if you look at the executive board of any business in the country, you are going to find at least one of us there and often they are the ones leading the business. Employers value the introvert because of the work and great ideas they can bring to the table, you just need to make sure that your value is not crumpled under the noise of those extroverts.

Social interactions used to be one of the hardest things to do. Going out when I had done a long day at work and talking to others and making new friends was the worse. But it is still nice to meet someone new and have some more friends, so getting through this in a way that works the best for the introvert is key. Just make sure that you do take a few nights off to yourself so that you can recharge and be your wonderful self in no time again.

Dating is another challenge that introverts can face in their lives, but this does not have to be an issue if you do not let it. I have dated many different people through my life, some were fellow introverts while others were extroverts and while it is sometimes hard to get out of your shell and learn something new, dating can lead to such wonderful experiences and you should not let your need to stay away from crowds ruin that for you. Find someone who embraces the unique you that you are and make some compromises and soon everyone is going to be happy with the arrangement.

Many people think that it is a bad thing to be an introvert, but what they do not notice is that even many famous people they already know and love are introverts who were able to use their skills and unique perspective of the world in order to become famous. Some well-known introverts would include Bill Gates, Abraham Lincoln, Albert Einstein, Audrey Hepburn, Warren Buffett, Gwyneth Paltrow, Julia Roberts, Barbara Walters, David Letterman, and Johnny Carson. These are names that most people would recognize for their acting, hosting, or running big companies, and yet they are introverts just like you. They didn't see being an introvert as something to run from but rather something to embrace in order to get where they wanted to go.

I do hope that this guidebook can be the help that you need to see that being an introvert is not something that is a bad thing nor does it have to make things in your life unduly difficult. Use it to find out just how amazing you are and come to the same realization that I did that being an introvert means that you are an amazing person.

Chapter 1: Why It is Actually Good to be an Introvert

The idea of being an introvert is something that has been looked down upon for a long time. There are a lot of people, especially those who are extroverts, who feel like the introvert is too shy and would rather go into a little cocoon and never talk to anyone. They might not see that there are a lot of benefits that can be found when you are being an introvert.

Just because you are an introvert does not mean that you are a shy little person who is just trying to get away from everyone else and wants nothing to do with them. It is just that you prefer to have things be a certain way and have a few close friends. Extroverts may like to be out and partying and know everyone, but how many of those people are actually close friends with them? On the other hand, the introvert is going to have just a few close friends they know really well and have known for a long time and they enjoy just having fun and a quiet life of their own. Neither is wrong, but there are just so many benefits that you will be able to see when it comes to being an introvert.

This section is going to spend some time talking about the top advantages of being an introvert. If you are considered an introvert, don't let the others bring you down and make you feel like you do not matter as much as them. Look at some of these cool advantages that only introverts are going to be able to enjoy.

1. Works well with the others around them. This is even truer when they are doing a relationship with someone that is one on one. They know how to get work done and since they are able to keep their heads level and not get too caught up in other things, they are very observant and are going to be able to notice important things about the other person that can make the relationship work so much better. Those who have worked with introverts in the past know that it is a great way to work because things get done and even though they are much quieter than

other people, it is easier to form a good connection with them.

2. Have friendships for the long term. Introverts are the kind of people who may take some time to make new friends, but once they have made one, they are going to be close to that person for a very long time. They may still have a friend from elementary school who they talk to years later. This is a great comfort to the introvert because they do not have to be surrounded by a lot of people as long as they are around some close friends they can always count on.

3. Flexible—introverts are able to be really flexible. They can see more than one way to get things done and something getting in the way and taking up a bit of time is not going to ruin their day. Some of the other personality types may flip out if a meeting comes up or they are not able to do something in a certain way because it will cut into their plants, they are really high strung, or they just do not have the right frame of mind to

get things on the track that they need to be on. None of this is true with the introvert who can stay calm and has the flexibility to work with others.

4. Independent—this is one that surprises a lot of people, but introverts are the ones who are the most independent in the world. They may not have a lot of connections in the world but they have the right connections to get things done. They may not talk a lot, but they can get things done quickly and on their own. Employers love having an introvert at work because they are not going to spend all day wasting time with talking and the boss does not have to stand over the introverts shoulder in order to get the work done.

5. Concentration. If you have ever watched an introvert spend some time on their work, you will be amazed at how deep in concentration they are able to get. They can focus on one task at a time and get the work done much more quickly than some of the other personality types who are going to spend time with thoughts going

through every part of their mind. This allows them to get the work done in no time and sets them up to have the free time they need.

6. Ability to reflect on the self. This might not seem like such a big deal to some, but it does allow the introvert to think about their life, the things that they have done, and the things that they would like to do in the future. This is going to serve them great because they are never going to get lost in what they would like to do and even though they may not want to go out and party like some other people, they are going to be the ones on top one day.

7. Responsible. Introverts are some of the most responsible people that you will meet. If they make a promise to do something, they are going to stick with it unless something way out of their control ends up getting in the way. They do not take on more than they can handle and always stay with what they promise because they take their responsibilities very seriously.

8. Creative and out of the box when it comes to thinking. Instead of just bouncing around or worrying about socializing with people, the introvert is often able to put that energy into thinking in a creative way. This is going to serve them so much in their life. First, being able to think in a creative way is going to help them out when they are working because no boss wants to be told ideas that have been floated around hundreds of times in the past. Plus it is a bonus to keep themselves busy and to having fun.

9. Analytical skills. Not only are introverts really creative and have great concentration skills, they also are able to have complex thoughts that have a lot of different things matched together. When other people see a complex problem and think that it is impossible to deal with, the introvert is going to be able to get it all fixed up in no time.

10. Smart and studious. Since the introvert likes to have some time to spend on their own and get things done, they are

often very smart. They will find the things that interest them or they will just study things in general and because they are just hanging out with those who are similar to them and bouncing ideas off each other, it is able to help them to learn even more. If you want to get a good grade on your next exam or project, it is best to work with someone who is an introvert because they are going to give you the best results.

These help to show that there are a lot of cool things that being an introvert is able to do for you. This is not something that you should be ashamed of being because there is often much more that you are going to be able to accomplish compared to other groups and some of the most successful people in the world are those who were considered introverts. Just look at all of the cool things that introverts can do and as soon as other personality types begin to look at it, they are going to be rushing to be your new best friend in order to get some of those benefits as well.

Chapter 2: How to be Successful in the Work Place

The work place is actually one of the places that the introvert is going to be able to shine the most when it comes to being successful. While some people may see them as shy or boring, they are the ones who are going to be the movers and the shakers of the whole world, even if their movements are much quieter than some of the other personality types. Just because you are an introvert does not mean that you do not have a chance to make it big in the work place.

Let's look at some of the numbers. It is estimated that at least a third of the population in America is considered introverts. This is a pretty big number to start with but the percentage goes even higher when you look at how many successful names in the business world are also considered to be introverts. These would include people like Marissa Mayer, Warren Buffet, Bill Gates, and Steve Wozniak among many others. Despite this, most people think that they need to change from being an introvert and instead conform to being like the extroverts around them in order to see any success.

This is often due to the fact that the business model of most businesses in this country are based off a model that seems to favor the extrovert, even if this might not be the best way to run things. You need to be able to talk loudly, get noticed, promote yourself if you want to be noticed, and make the right connections quickly. These are things that the extrovert is able to do better than the introvert, but some of the talents that the introvert possesses, like thinking skills, being able to concentrate, and doing well with one on one tasks, are much better to being in charge in the business world. This makes it really confusing for the introvert; they are trying to figure out if they should be themselves or if they should work towards being like the extroverts who always seem to get the breaks.

Despite all of this, it is still possible to be really successful at the work place even when you are being true to yourself and being an introvert. While it might not seem like it with all of the noise that comes from the extroverts, it is possible to make it big when you are the introvert and with the right steps, you are going to do better than everyone else in the building. The following are some of the steps that you can take in order to shine when you are at the work place.

Embrace the thoughts

Introverts are often the ones who are going to sit down in the meetings and be quiet. This does not mean that they are ignoring what is being said or that they do not care, rather, they are listening to the arguments from both sides so that they are able to form the opinion based on what they hear. When they do chime into the conversation, they are able to add in some thoughtful comments as well as a perspective that might be a bit more balanced than what others have been saying. Do not feel like you need to chime in just because everyone else is. Take the time to think before you say something, but also do not be shy to make a contribution when you have something. Remember that your one insightful comment can make a bigger impact than all of the jabbering that is going on around you.

Prepare

Most introverts like to be prepared for any presentation and meeting that they may be going to. They do not like to just try and wing it. There are a few benefits to doing this. First you are going to show that you are very passionate about the work that you are doing and that it is important enough to you to think it all through rather than just hoping it all works out. The next benefit is that you are giving yourself enough time to get the right facts ahead of time and get them all organized before you have to talk to someone else. This preparation can help you to see some potential issues that could have been missed at a last minute presentation style and you can even propose some solutions that will get you on the top. Stick with this need to prepare and you will be able to go far.

Play with the strengths

All introverts have some strengths that are all their own and you should make sure that you are using these to your advantage. For example, a lot of introverts like to write out things rather than speak their minds. Use this kind of gift to promote the expertise as well as enthusiasm that you have for something. Try out some social media, blogging, and some other options that can help you to get your ideas out there and could even give you the dream job that you have been looking for.

Keep the calm

In the business world, it is easy for everyone to get in a fuss about nothing and the emotions can get high in no time. When it comes to the introvert, it is much easier to keep their emotions in check no matter what the situation may be. These people are going to be reserved and calm. When everything is moving around them so quickly, being able to stay calm and figure out the situation before responding is a big advantage in the business world. If you spend the time to act calmly, those around you will start to feel like everything is fine and they are going to trust you. This starts to sound a lot like a leader and hopefully your boss is able to recognize this and give you the reward that you deserve.

Keep the alone time

Introverts, despite being able to stay calm and take care of the things that are going on in their lives, can get really overwhelmed with the things that go on around them. This is why they need to have some of the precious alone time that can help them to recharge. Some introverts feel like they should get out and be more social with others in order to get ahead, this is not going to do them any good if they are worn out and just need to be alone. Respect this time; this is the time that you need in order to rest and be the amazing person that you appear at work every day. There are a lot of ways that you can get your quiet time whether it is going out for a quick walk at lunch, shutting the office door for just a minute or two during the day, or just spending a night home alone and reading your favorite book.

These quiet moments are not going to be easy to find in the business world, but you need to take as many of them as you can as an introvert so that you can recharge and show off how great of a person that you are. This allows you to get refreshed, energized, and all ready to get going on the new challenges in your life. Do not feel guilty because you do not want to spend every second of every day socializing and being everyone's best friend; that is not who you are and trying to be that way is just going to cause you a lot of harm.

Build the right connections

Extroverts have a strategy of gong around and making a lot of connections in a short period of time. They think that the more connections that they have the better it is for them to get ahead. The issue with this is that they might end up making some of the wrong connections in their haste and often there are just too many people for them to be in contact with that they are missing out on opportunities even if they knew the right person.

While it would be much more fun to sit at home and read a good book or watch a good movie, going out and networking every once in a while is a great way to open your borders and get you ahead in the work place. You do not have to do this all of the time, but a few times is great. You do not have to add pressure to yourself by comparing how well you are doing compared to others in terms of numbers. Instead, make a goal of meeting one or two new people who are going to form deep relationships with you and who will be able to be the best connections for your purpose. Even if you just make two new connections, meeting with the head of the department you would like to transfer over to be going to get you much further than just talking to the guy who fills the vending machine.

Show the passion

Introverts can really show the passion like no other when they find something that really interest them. You may not like to show it off too much with small talk, but then you can just turn it on to be about something that really is passionate to you rather than do the small talk. Talking may be difficult for you to do, but if you are able to show the passion that you have for something, you can show off another side that no one has seen before.

Even if it is not something that you are all that passionate about, use some of your skills of working with others and writing to at least show that you are enthusiastic about the job at hand. This allows the others around you to see that you are happy in your work and your job and they are going to really appreciate this. You should do this kind of enthusiasm for the emails that you are sending, when you talk to your boss, or you are talking to a client. When you show some genuine enthusiasm, the ones around you will begin to take notice.

Remember that success comes from the inside

You need to remember that in order to succeed in the business world, you need to let others know what you are bringing to the table. Even as an introvert, you have some unique talents, skills, and other things that are going to help out the business that no one else is going to have. But since the extroverts are making all of the noise, it is easy for the boss to get lost in all of that and not remember that you are there and making the biggest contribution out of them all. You need to bring it to their attention in order to get the recognition that you need.

Never let the qualities that you have as an introvert seem like they are obstacles to the success that you want to get. Rather, these are the things that are going to put you ahead of everyone else in the business world. You are a great introvert who can bring a lot to the table and you just need to let others know about it as well and you are soon going to see the success that you have been dreaming of.

Chapter 3: Being the Introvert in Social Interactions

Even though you are an introvert, you can still go out in public and make a lot of friend and new acquaintances. Unlike those who are considered extroverts, you may not meet everyone who is at the party, but that does not mean that you are not able to have a great time and make some meaningful connections. Here are some of the ways that you can be social while still remaining true to your introvert self.

Making New Friends

Making new friends as an introvert is hard. You want to make sure that someone is worth your time before you start to share details with them or become their friend, but most people do not want to wait around that long to give you the chance. The ones who do can become some of your best friends and you will always have your back, but most people just want to have a lot of people they know and not a lot of real close friends. Even as an introvert you are able to make some great friends, it just may take a bit longer than it does for other people. Here are some of the steps that you can do as an introvert in order to make some of the best friends you will ever meet while having fun with social interactions.

Find a hobby

Even as an introvert, you are going to have a hobby that you like to do. Some people like to read, others like to fish, shop, go on walks, workout, visit art museums, craft, and so much more. Introverts can like to do anything that other people like to do. You probably already know your hobby and this is a great place to start if you would like to make new friends. If you are out doing the hobby and see someone who likes to do it to, why not spend some time making a new friend? It is not fun to have a friend who shares no interests in common with you so find something that you can both enjoy doing and see how easy the friendship can come for the both of you.

Seize the moment

While it is fine to be an introvert and a little withdrawn, you do need to seize the moment at some time if you would like to make some new friends. If you are working on a big project with others, take the chance to talk with them or see if they would like to go out after the project to get some coffee. If someone new just moved into the neighborhood, go over and say hello and let them know that you would be available if they have questions or need something while they are getting settled.

These simple tasks are sometimes hard for the introvert to do. They are used to being on their own and they may not know how to make the first move. This can be a little bit scary but you are never going to make new friends if you do not get out there a bit and start just by saying hello. Just remember, social people are not crazy or aliens and the only way for you to make the new friends that you would like is to go out there and meet them.

Try something funny

There is no better way for breaking the ice then to get them to laugh over something. This is one of the things that can get people talking, feeling better about their day, and they will feel like they are bonding together better. It is also a good way to start up a new conversation so this can help out if you are not sure what to say to those around you during the party. Just keep in mind that there is appropriate funny and then there is the funny that can get you in trouble so just remember who is in the company you are talking with before you get started. You should also never laugh at others because this is going to make you look like you are petty and mean, which is not a good way to make some new friends.

Keep in contact

Sometimes an introvert is going to forget that they need to keep in contact with their friends. This is not because they do not like their friends or mean to forget, but they like to have some nights off alone and when you have work and school and other obligations, it is hard to find the time to fit in the alone nights with the nights you should fit in with friends. While introverts may love their friends, they will often choose to spend the night in on their own and enjoy something in peace.

But if you want to make friends and keep them around, you need to remember to contact them on occasion. Ignoring your friends, whether they are old ones or new ones, is going to drive them away because they do not want to be your friend any longer. Call them up, ask them over for dinner, and send them a little gift when it is Christmas time. It is a lot of work for someone who is an introvert to make friends so why waste all of that time if you just quit talking to them and lose the friendships you have made. You do not have to hang out with them all of the time though, having those alone nights on occasion are still fine, just do not forget about your friends all of the time.

Never Lie

No one wants to be friends with someone who is going to lie to them all of the time. If you are being fake, others are going to notice it and they will start to wonder if you want to hang out with them or not. Someone who is considered a good companion will be someone that you want to be with. If you do not feel comfortable around someone, it is not a good idea to make friends with them. As an introvert, you are going to be able to tell if someone is worth your time or if you feel comfortable with someone pretty early on. Do not try to force yourself to get along with someone you are not liking just because you think you need more friends.

Also, you should not lie in the sense of telling someone that you are doing one thing and really you are doing something else. Some introverts may find that they are becoming friends with someone who is an extrovert. After some time going out all of the time, they may feel tired and like they need to recharge for a bit. Instead of lying and saying you are not feeling good or that you have a lot of work to do, just let your friend know that you need a day off and you can catch up the next time. This is going to get you a lot further in the long run and they will appreciate that you were honest with them.

Be Yourself

No matter how much you want to make friends and have a social life, if you are not able to be yourself, then it is not worth it. Remember that you are a unique person who has wants and needs just like anyone else and if others are stomping all over you, they are not your friends and you should move on to someone else. Have an opinion, be the equal of your friends, and realize that a fight might come up on occasion with a friend, but that is fine because this shows that you both have an opinion. Never let anyone tell you how to act or make you feel like being the quieter and more relaxed introvert is such a bad thing.

Large Social Gatherings

As an introvert, large social gatherings can be really difficult to deal with. There are going to be a lot of people going around and making noise and just looking at it all can end up kind of exhausting. No one wants to deal with all of this as an introvert, but you do have to get out there and learn how to be comfortable on occasion. The following are some of the things that you can do as an introvert at parties in order to get out there and socializing while also making new friends.

Just go and do it

Introverts may find that it is hard to get out and do something. They like to be in their little comfort zones where they can think things through and know everyone around them. But this is not how you are going to make a lot of new friends or get through the large social gatherings. When you are at these events, just remember that these are all new faces who have not had a chance to determine who you are or what you are all about. It is up to you to tell them who this person is and why they should like you.

Do not see this as a challenge or something to be scared about. Yes keeping up with everything can be scary, but if you are just true to yourself and keep on trying, you are going to be much better. You will find that there are a ton of new people to get to know around you and if you are just spending the time on each person individually rather than looking at them like they are part of a huge crowd, it can be more fun and the time will pass much more quickly.

Relax and get yourself comfortable

Being all tensed up is not going to help the situation and it is going to make the whole thing more likely that you will tense up and say something that you did not want or mean to day. Instead, you need to find a way to go to some of these parties without being all weirded out or worried before you get there.

There are several ways that you can do this. First, while you are at the party, just realize that everyone is there to have a good time. They are not there to judge you or to point out all of the flaws that you have. Many social gatherings are just excuses to have a lot of fun so have some with everyone else and it is going to be so much better. Some introverts find that being relaxed and happy before they leave the house can make them feel better. If a big project has you stressed out from work, it is not a good idea to head to the party feeling all tense. Watch a funny show, dance around to some music, workout, or do something else that is able to reduce the anxiety and stress you are feeling and which is going to get you back on the right setting for the party. When you are relaxed, you are not going to worry about things as much and then you will find that the party is much more fun and it is easier to talk to those around you.

Set a goal

If you have some issues with meeting and making new friends when you are in social gatherings, it might be a good idea to set some goals that are pretty simple. Perhaps you can make a goal to talk to two new people at the party. They can be any two people you would like but you need to make sure that you are talking to at least that many during the event. You can slowly add it up to three or four people during each event until you are talking to as many as you feel comfortable with. You do not have to go crazy with this, just make sure that you are meeting new people no matter the situation.

Get help

In some cases, you are already going to have some friends who are pretty outgoing and already know how to make a lot of friends on their own. Use these friends if you can in order to make it easier to have some of your own friends. They can help you out in so many ways with this. First they can cheer you on and give you the encouragement that you need in order to get out there and meet new people. Another way they can help is to perhaps introduce you to some of the people they already know. This can make things easier because you will have a person in common to talk about and then you can avoid the random and awkward introductions that come with just walking up to a new person. Either way, this is going to help you to get to the goals you are making.

Do not run from the nerves

It is normal to feel a bit nervous when you are meeting new people. You are not sure how they are going to react to you or if you are going to like them at all. This is normal and a good sign that you are alive so do not be scared of these nerves but rather embrace them. Socialization, especially for a true introvert, is not going to come with just one try and often it is going to take quite a few of them. In spite of these nerves, stretch out to the boundaries and slowly start to move them so that you are comfortable in more situations. Do not worry if someone you have met once is not sure of how you acted or you embarrassed yourself in front of them. If they minded a lot then you do not want to be friends and for the most part, they will have barely noticed or will appreciate the time you took. Soon you will learn how to banter and do small talk better and these new social interactions will become a lot more fun.

Make the conversation about the other person

Most introverts are not going to want to spend a lot of time talking about themselves. Of course, if someone asks you a direct question about yourself, it would be rude not to answer, but if this is making you a bit uncomfortable, the best strategy that you can employ is to answer the questions and then turn it back so it becomes more about them. This is going to work in two ways. First you are going to take some of the attention from yourself, which is the ultimate goal since introverts are not likely to want to talk all day about themselves. Next, instead of looking like a selfish thing to do, it is showing that you are really interested in the other person and what they have to say. And the other person, especially if they are an extrovert, is going to love having the chance to talk all about themselves to someone who is interested. It is going to be a win-win for all who are involved.

Using these tips to help out at major parties and other social events that you are at can be a great way to ensure that you are still meeting some of the new people that you would like but in a method that is going to work for you being the way that you are. You have nothing wrong with you, it is just important to learn the ways that work best so that you are comfortable and actually have the best chance in the room of making some new friends and having a lot of fun. Try out some of this tricks today to learn just how much fun it can be to make some new friends as an introvert any time you are ready.

Chapter 4: Dating as an Introvert

As an introvert, you may find the idea of dating one that is really scary. You may have been told that it is impossible or since you have so much trouble with social interactions, you are worried that you will not be able to find someone who is willing to stick it out with you and learn how great of a person you really are.

But dating as an introvert does not have to be as big of a deal as you think. It can be a great experience that allows you to meet some new people, learn more about yourself, and perhaps meet the one who is your soul mate. Just because you do not like to socialize all of the time does not mean that you are not able to find someone you like being with and who can accept you the way that you are. This chapter is going to look a bit on the idea of dating as an introvert to show you just how easy it can really be.

Tips for Dating

If you are not used to dating and you are an introvert, that first date is going to seem like something that is difficult to do. You may start to feel anxious and nervous and wonder if you are going to be able to get through it. First off, take a few deep breaths and get those thoughts about the person you are dating not liking you out of your head. You are a great catch and anyone is going to be lucky to have you. But if you are still a bit nervous, here are some of the steps that you can take in order to make sure that this is a great experience for the both of you on date night:

1. Be truthful—let your date know right away that you are not the most social person and that you actually prefer a night in with take out and a movie rather than going out to the clubs. This is going to work out in two ways. First, if the person does not appreciate that and does not want to do it with you, then you dodged a bullet before you got too attached. Second, you may find out that the only reason your date wanted to go to the club and be out all

of the time is because they were trying to make you happy and give you a good time, but they would love to just stay in and talk as well. If the latter is true, you probably just found your soulmate. Be honest from the beginning and your dating experience is going to be so much better.

2. Meet where you will be comfortable—if you are a person who does not like loud places, do not go there. While being an introvert is going to make you more of a people please, you need to remember that the whole dating experience is supposed to be pleasant and if you are not having any fun, the other person will be able to tell and you will not be able to learn more about them or have a good date. Take the time to suggest a place that will make you a bit more comfortable, such as a coffee shop or the park.

3. Avoid the smooth talkers—you are too smart for this and can probably spot a fake a mile away. The issue might be that you are so anxious that you jump in with the first person who will go on

a date with you that the smooth talker ends up getting in on the date. For a relationship to work, you will need to find someone who is willing to hear you and give you time to speak, something that is not going to happen with the person who is just going to talk the whole time without letting you in at all.

4. Look for the connection that is more subtle—sometimes the first impressions that you are getting are going to be so strong that you are going to have some issues with feeling how the person really is. Sure they may talk a big talk or look and smell nice, but take a second to think how it would be like to just sit and talk to them for an hour or two. This is what you will be doing on the date and if the thought already bores you or you know you will not have a good time, it is probably the best to skip out on this kind of date. You want to have a good time, especially on the first few dates, so make sure that you are going to

have a good chance at a good time with them before getting started.

5. Beware of those who always take—as an introvert, you are the kind of person who is often going to be giving all of the time to those around you. The introvert is good at listening, paying attention, and being there for others. While this is a great thing to have in a relationship, it is never going to work if the other person is never going to give some of it back to you. No matter how much you would like to, it is not fair to just sit there and give and give to the other person who is never giving anything back. If you have to sit there and ask for them to do something for you or to include you in something, you may already have your sign that this is not going somewhere that is good for you.

Dating as an introvert can sometimes present its own challenges, but this does not mean that you should run away from it or not enjoy it. Introverts can have just as much fun dating as anyone else, they just have to take some extra time to make sure they are finding someone who is just right for them. These tips above can help to make this possible.

Dating an Extrovert: Can it Work?

So another question that many introverts may ask is whether they are able to just date other introverts or if they should take a chance with someone who is an extrovert. This is a good question that has a lot of debate going around, and often it is going to depend on the kind of person. Sometimes it is good to date an introvert because they are going to understand you a bit better, but if they are too boring and want to stay home by themselves rather than hanging out with you, they are not a good match. On the other hand, dating an extrovert who always wants to party and go out is probably not the best for you, but if you can come up with a compromise of staying in sometimes and going out other times, the relationship can work. It all just depends on the situation.

This does not mean that there are not going to be a few setbacks along the way if you are dating an extrovert. You both are going to run into some disagreements and not be able to decide on who gets to pick the activity for the night and so on. This is no indication that it is not going to work between the two of you, it just means that you are going to have to put in the work to find out how to stay together.

Here are some tips that the both of you can enjoy in order to make sure that the relationship is going to last for the long term when dating an extrovert.

Define needs

You need to be able to define the needs that you have to your partner so that they are able to understand what is going on. Your partner will need to do the same. You might find that when an extrovert says they want to go out, you are going to have visions of loud music and tons of people that you do not know while they just thought going for a walk outside and seeing the sights while getting supper was a good idea. The first one would probably put you into panic attacks while the second one would be much more acceptable to you. But acting like the first one was the only choice is going to probably lead to a fight. Both of you need to be able to list more than just few word answers for some results.

You need to speak out as well. With the other example, if your partner does want to go out and you do not, instead of just saying you don't you can consider saying that you just are not up for crowds or a lot of noise tonight. This still leaves the possibility for the walk and fresh air idea listed above while still letting your partner get out of the house like they need.

Define the boundaries

This needs to be done early on in your relationship so that both people can understand what is going on. For example, while you may be an introvert you are fine with meeting new people at times, it just depends on the situation. You may not like going to a place that has all of your partners friends, none of whom know you or seem that interested in knowing you, but you are fine going on a double date with a few friends you both know. Your partner will need to be honest about their feelings as well. They might be fine with staying in and watching a movie or reading with you, but they would not like to stay in and just have no plans all of the time. Defining which situations are good for the other is imperative if you would like to have success in this relationship.

Make some quality time

No matter what kind of relationship you are in and with whom, having some time that is just for the two of you is important. The issue that comes up is that the extrovert and the introvert are going to have different ideas of what this quality time means. You might have to split up this time a bit to make both people happy. While you might love watching a movie or going on a long walk, your partner might want to go out bowling or hang out with a couple of mutual friends on occasion. Have a compromise in place that goes back and forth so that the both of you can have the time that you need together doing things you both love.

Make friends together

While each of you are going to have your own friends that you brought into the relationship to start with, it is also good to make some friends together. This does not mean that you have to give up the friends you already have, but you can go out and do things together and make friends in that way as well. This is going to work out well for you because you already have your partner around who is good at making friends and who is going to make it easier for you to make some too. This can also give you some common stories to share, someone to go do things together, and can make your relationship just that much stronger because you made the friends together.

Check that the other is having fun

Just because it is your time to make the decision on what to do or where to go, does not mean that you would want your partner to be completely bored during the whole thing. This experience is supposed to be about having fun together so try to be considerate of that. If they are bored with that whole marathon you want to watch, save it for one of the nights that you are alone and maybe watch a movie that you both wanted to see or go out and get some ice cream. They will hopefully be just as considerate of you when the time comes and this can make the relationship so much stronger.

As you can see, it is possible to have a great relationship with someone who is an extrovert when you are an introvert, it is just going to take a little bit of time and effort from both parties in order to accomplish it. Both sides are going to need to work to be caring and considerate of the other person; if they are successful then the relationship is going to do well and they will both be happy but if they are not successful, the relationship is going to end up failing in no time. Working together is going to ensure that the both of you are in a relationship that is really strong and that you will both have a lot of fun and get something meaningful out of it at the same time.

Conclusion

Being an introvert is not something that you should be ashamed of or that you should let others talk you out of. This is who you are and if you are able to embrace it, like I did, you are going to see that it can bring you a lot of amazing things in your life. As you can see, an introvert is able to do anything that someone else does, they just need to be able to do it on their own terms and it is going to work out great. Use this guidebook that I have presented to you in order to learn how to navigate some of the toughest parts about being an introvert and soon things will turn out even better than you could have ever imagined in your life.

Check Out My Other Books

If you like this book, make sure to check out some of my other books. These include:

- Reinventing Your Life: Be the Change You Want to See
  http://www.amazon.com/Reinventing-Your-Life-Change-Want-ebook/dp/B00V556NR8/ref=asap_bc?ie=UTF8

- The Gluten-Free Cookbook: 40 Fun, Simple & Delicious Everyday Recipes
  http://www.amazon.com/Gluten-Free-Cookbook-Delicious-Everyday-Recipes-ebook/dp/B00TZ98EQY/ref=sr_1_5?ie=UTF8&qid=1433865068&sr=8-5&keywords=kendra+wilson

www.ingramcontent.com/pod-product-compliance
Lightning Source LLC
Chambersburg PA
CBHW070827290526
45795CB00002B/865